THE Daily Meow

Written by Jill Eggleton
Illustrated by Richard Hoit

Cat Robber
Raids Again

The cat robber has been in Nob Street again. Fat Cat was asleep by his dinner when it was snatched from under his nose. The cat robber did not leave any paw prints. This is the third time the cat robber has snatched food from Fat Cat. The people in Nob Street have to feed their cats inside. They have to keep all their doors shut.

Tiger Trio at Cat Concert

The Tiger Trio were playing their drums at the Cat Ball on Saturday. Cats from everywhere came to the ball. It was a very warm night. There was no wind and the moon was big and bright. The Tiger Trio were very good players. The cats were waving their tails and clapping their paws all night.

FLU HITS FAT CATS

The fat cats on Nob Hill have all had the cat flu. The vet said "fat cats who sleep by the fire and then go out late at night catch cold and get the cat flu". The cat flu is not very nice. Cats get red eyes and they sneeze and sneeze. Some fat cats have lost their meow.

No Scraps For Alley Cats

The alley cats that live under the shops are hungry. The shopkeepers are not putting any food in the rubbish bins. One shopkeeper said that everyone should put food in their bins. He said, "The alley cats do a good job of chasing away the rats. If we don't look after the alley cats, we will have millions of rats in our street. People will not want to come to our shops."

First Prize Awarded to Marmalade

Marmalade has taken first prize in the annual cat show held on Sunday. The judges said Marmalade's clean fur was wonderful. They thought she must have been licking it for weeks. Marmalade got a blue ribbon, ten fat chops, and a big box of ice cream. Her owner, Jo Brown, was very pleased.

News Flash: Police are looking for Womcat. Womcat is not in his house in Dogsville. He was last seen by the river. He was walking across the bridge.

Birdwatch Column

The parrots are back in the park. The cats from the Birdwatch Club said they had seen six red parrots with long green tails in the trees. All cats in the park are being told to look out for these parrots. The parrots like to dive-bomb any cat that walks in the park by itself.

Newspaper Reports

Newspaper reports tell the reader about new, important, unusual or interesting information.

A newspaper report begins with the most important part of the story — the headline.

Cat Robber Raids Again

The headline gets the reader's attention and tells about the main idea of the news story.

FLU HITS FAT CATS

No Scraps For Alley Cats

Next comes the **introduction**.

An introduction needs to keep the reader's attention.

Introductions should be short.
Introductions should tell the readers about:

What happened

To who

When and where

The **rest of the report** is about more facts!

News reports are usually about one thing.

They should not give an opinion.

▬▬ **Guide Notes**

Title: The Daily Meow
Stage: Launching Fluency

Text Form: Newspaper Report
Approach: Guided Reading
Processes: Thinking Critically, Exploring Language, Processing Information
Written and Visual Focus: Newspaper Reports, Headlines, Columns of Type

---

THINKING CRITICALLY
(sample questions)
- What do you think is the most important news? Why ?
- What do you think is the most humorous news? Why?
- Where would the reporter have to be to get the news about the alley cats?
- What news item would you like to find out more about?
- What news did you find the most interesting? Why?
- Do you think the reports in this book are true/not true? Why/why not?

EXPLORING LANGUAGE

Terminology
Spread, author and illustrator credits, ISBN number

Vocabulary
Clarify: trio, alley, annual, dive-bomb
Nouns: cats, rats, shopkeeper, show
Verbs: snatch, sneeze, clean, look
Singular/plural: print/prints, tail/tails, bin/bins, shop/shops

Print Conventions
Apostrophes – possessive (Marmalade's clean fur), contraction (don't)

Phonological Patterns
Focus on short and long vowel **e** (g**e**t, r**e**d, h**e**ld, t**e**n, asl**ee**p, s**ee**n, str**ee**t)
Discuss base words – waving, clapping, putting
Look at suffix **ful** (wonder**ful**)